IF I RAN the RAIN FOREST

I'm the Cat in the Hat
and it's time that we get
to go to a place
that is steamy and wet.

The Cat in the Hat's Learning Library™ introduces beginning readers to basic non-fiction. If your child can read these lines, then he or she can begin to understand the fascinating world in which we live.

Learn to read. Read to learn.

This book comes from the home of

THE CAT IN THE HAT

RANDOM HOUSE, INC.

*For a list of books in **The Cat in the Hat's Learning Library**, see the back endpaper.*

The editors would like to thank
BARBARA KIEFER, Ph.D.,
Associate Professor of Reading and Literature,
Teachers College, Columbia University, and
JIM BREHENY, Director, Bronx Zoo Special Animal Exhibits and Operations,
Wildlife Conservation Society,
for their assistance in the preparation of this book.

www.randomhouse.com/seussville

Library of Congress Cataloging-in-Publication Data
Worth, Bonnie. If I ran the rain forest / by Bonnie Worth ; illustrated by Aristides Ruiz.
  p. cm. — (The Cat in the Hat's learning library)
SUMMARY: In rhyming text, the Cat in the Hat introduces the tropical rain forest and the
ways in which its plants and animals interact.
ISBN 0-375-81097-8 (trade) — ISBN 0-375-91097-2 (lib. bdg.)
1. Rain forest ecology—Juvenile literature. 2. Rain forest animals—Juvenile literature.
3. Rain forest plants—Juvenile literature. 4. Rain forests—Juvenile literature.
[1. Rain forests. 2. Rain forest animals. 3. Rain forest plants. 4. Rain forest ecology.
5. Ecology.] I. Ruiz, Aristides, ill. II. Title. III. Series. QH541.5.R27 W67 2003
577.34—dc21 2002069804

Printed in the United States of America First Edition 10 9 8 7 6 5 4 3

IF I RAN
the
RAIN FOREST

by Bonnie Worth
illustrated by Aristides Ruiz

The Cat in the Hat's Learning Library™

Random House 🏠 New York

I'm the Cat in the Hat
and it's time that we get
to go to a place
that is steamy and wet.

It is a rain forest.
The reason is clear.
About one hundred inches
of rain falls each year.

Down at the equator
I'll show it to you.
Your mother won't mind
very much if I do.

EQUATOR

RAIN FOREST

BRAZIL

To a tropical rain forest
off we will go!
There are three other kind
I think you should know.

The seasonal kind
has months that are dry.
A cloud rain forest
sits three thousand feet high.

A mangrove rain forest
grows on the coast.
Rain falls on the tropical
rain forest most.

Dear Sally and Dick,
for your information,
the reason it's rainy
is called tran-spi-ra-tion.

TRANSPIRATION

- Plants lose water through pores in their leaves.

- Warm, wet air rises into the sky.

- Wet air cools and forms rain clouds.

- Plants soak up rain through their roots.

A rain forest has
four floors, you might say.
We'll visit each one,
so please step this way.

My umbrella-vator
will give the best view.
To the uppermost floor
it will take me and you.

12

E-mer-gents is the word
that we use to call
these trees that grow up
three hundred feet tall.

4TH floor:
EMERGENTS

They might be quite tall,
but I'm here to report
their roots don't go deep,
but they still give support.

Buttress roots grow
aboveground like a fan
to keep trees from falling.
That is Nature's plan.

Who makes their home here?
Those who like heights best . . .

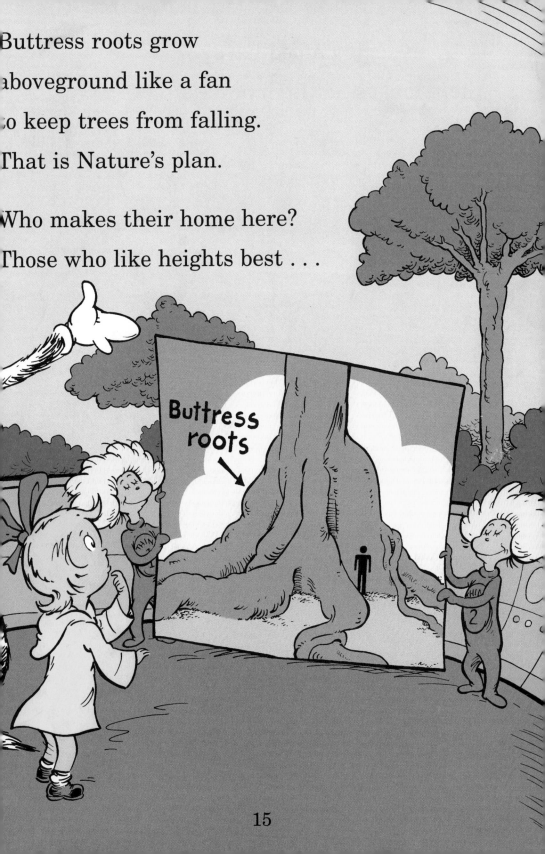

Buttress
roots

. . . an eagle named harpy
here makes her high nest.

This gaggle of parrots
of colorful hue
are macaws of scarlet
and yellow and blue.

Now we will go
down to floor three,
where lower treetops
form the green canopy.

It keeps rain and sun
off the floors down below.
It's also the place where
the e-pi-phytes grow.

These plants have roots
that hang here and there.
They suck up the moisture
right out of the air!

HOWLER MONKEYS

LIANAS

SLOTHS

TOUCANS

The canopy is
the most crowded of spots.
Here monkeys and tree frogs
and birds can eat lots
of fruits, nuts, and bugs
and the nectar of flowers.

ORCHIDS

TREE FROGS

It is NOISY round here,
and it's busy all hours!

Some animals here,
I have just found,
live their whole lives
without touching the ground!

RED-EYED
TREE FROGS

The wet leaves are slippery.
Movement is tricky.
And that's why their toes
and their fingers are sticky.

In the canopy—hark!

The hummingbirds hum.

Over two hundred kinds.

That is quite a large sum!

The hummingbird sips
at the nectar from blooms.
From flower to flower,
it flits and it zooms.

This little bird helps
the flowers to grow
because pollen sticks
to its body, and so . . .
when the pollen gets brushed
from its feet and its head,
it causes the pollen
to scatter and spread.

pitcher plants

This plant gives an insect
a most deadly ride.
It slips when it sips
and gets trapped inside.

strangler fig

If this plant can't root,

it will grow on another.

The vines twine and squeeze

and then, finally, smother!

The understory is
the next stop: floor two.
I'm afraid not much sun
can make its way through.

These vines and ferns grow
where it's dim and it's hot.
Spider monkey lives here,
and the wild ocelot.

Cam-ou-flage is the word
to describe a design
that makes things blend in
and so hard to find.

Find six hidden things
and you'll win a prize.
The sure way to win
is to sharpen your eyes.

31

Last stop: the first floor.
The doors open wide.
And when we look out,
it is quite dark outside!

Is anyone home?
At first, you'd say not.
There's mostly leaf litter,
dead plants, and some rot.

But jaguars prowl,
snakes slink and they slither.
Insects and spiders
creep yon and hither.

Now look even closer
and you will find
among the life here . . .

... is our own humankind!

For thousands of years,

they've lived here unharmed.

They've hunted and some

of them even have farmed.

They know where to find
the food for a meal.
They know which plants poison.
They know which plants heal.

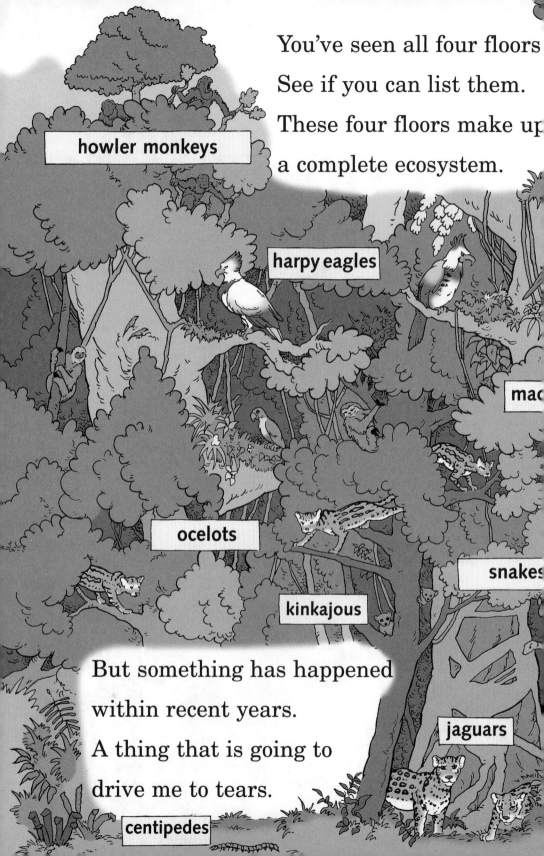

You've seen all four floors
See if you can list them.
These four floors make up
a complete ecosystem.

howler monkeys

harpy eagles

mac

ocelots

snakes

kinkajous

jaguars

But something has happened
within recent years.
A thing that is going to
drive me to tears.

centipedes

eaglets

Millions of acres
of land every year
are cut down for reasons
too long to list here.

spider monkeys

toucans

sloths

native human

If I ran the rain forest,
you know what I'd do?
I'd make a few changes.
That's just what I'd do.

GLOSSARY

Acre: A piece of land that was originally equal to the area that a team of oxen could plow in one day. An acre is about the size of a football field.

Buttress: To support or hold up.

Camouflage: To hide by blending in or being disguised.

Ecosystem: A group of animals and plants that live together as a single unit.

Emergent: A tall tree that pokes through the forest canopy.

Epiphyte: An air plant that thrives on the branches or trunk of another plant.

Equator: An imaginary circle running around the earth that lies an equal distance from the North and South Poles.

Hither and yon: An old-time way to say "here and there."

Hue: A shade of color.

Nectar: The sweet liquid found inside flowers, which bees use to make honey.

Pollen: The fine dust found inside flowers, which helps them reproduce new flowers.

Smother: To stop a living thing from breathing by covering or strangling.

Transpiration: The process in which plants lose water through pores in their leaves called "stomata." As water is lost from the plant, the plant takes up more water through its roots.

FOR FURTHER READING

Amazon Fever by Kathleen Weidner Zoehfeld, illustrated by Paulette Bogan (Random House, into Reading, Step 4). A boy and his uncle learn about the rain forest while searching for butter during a trip to the Amazon. For grades 2 and u

The Great Kapok Tree: A Tale of the Amazon Rain Forest by Lynne Cherry (Harcourt/Gulliver Rain forest creatures convince a woodcutter not cut down a tree. For preschoolers and up.

Nature's Green Umbrella: Tropical Rain Forests Gail Gibbons (William Morrow & Co.). Facts and illustrations teach all about the rain forest. For grades 2 and up.

The Rain Forest created by Gallimard Jeunesse and René Mettler, illustrated by René Mettler (Scholastic, A First Discovery Book). An introdu to the plants and animals of the rain forest. For preschoolers and up.

Red-Eyed Tree Frog by Joy Cowley, photographe Nic Bishop (Scholastic). Color photos follow the adventures of a rain forest tree frog searching f something to eat. For preschoolers and up.

INDEX

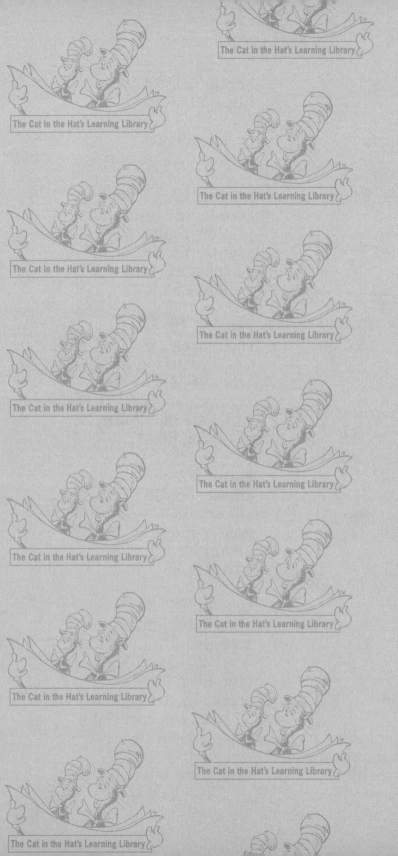

The Cat in the Hat's Learning Library™

Fine Feathered Friends
A Great Day for Pup
If I Ran the Rain Forest
Is a Camel a Mammal?
Oh Say Can You Say DI-NO-SAUR?
Oh Say Can You Seed?
Oh, the Things You Can Do
That Are Good for You!
On Beyond Bugs!
There's a Map on My Lap!
There's No Place Like Space!
Wish for a Fish

Coming in Fall 2003:

Inside Your Outsides